Introducing Continents

South America

Anita Ganeri

Raintree is an imprint of Capstone Global Library Limited, a company incorporated in England and Wales having its registered office at 7 Pilgrim Street, London, EC4V 6LB – Registered company number: 6695582

To contact Raintree, please phone 0845 6044371, fax + 44 (0) 1865 312263, or email myorders@ raintreepublishers.co.uk.

Edited by Dan Nunn, Rebecca Rissman, Sian Smith, and Helen Cox Cannons
Designed by Philippa Jenkins
Original illustrations © Capstone Global Library Ltd 2014
Picture research by Liz Alexander and Tristan Leverett
Production by Vicki Fitzgerald
Originated by Capstone Global Library Ltd
Printed and bound in China by Leo Paper Products Ltd

ISBN 978 1 406 26299 5
17 16 15 14
10 9 8 7 6 5 4 3 2

British Library Cataloguing in Publication Data
Ganeri, Anita
Introducing South America. – (Introducing continents)
A full catalogue record for this book is available from the British Library.

Acknowledgements
We would like to thank the following for permission to reproduce photographs: Alamy p. 16 (© Les Gibbon); Corbis pp. 7 (© Johannes Mann), 18 (© Kit Houghton), 23 (© Peter M. Wilson); Getty Images pp. 14 (Paul Souders/The Image Bank), 22 (Alejandro Pagni/AFP); naturepl.com p. 17 (© Juan Manuel Borrero); Science Photo Library pp. 9 (Jacques Jangoux), 10 (Jacques Jangoux); Shutterstock pp. 6 (© Andrés Cuenca), 8 (© Natursports), 11 (© colacat), 12 (© XuRa), 13 (© Peter Zaharov), 15 (© Rechitan Sorin), 26 (© cifotart); SuperStock pp. 19 (Jan Sochor/age footstock), 20 (Prisma), 21 (Tips Images), 25 (imagebroker.net), 27 (Michael &Amp Jennifer Lewis/National Geographic).

Cover image of a shaded relief map of South America reproduced with permission of Shutterstock (© AridOcean); images of the Amazon River, Brazil and carnival parade at the Sambodrome, Rio de Janeiro, Brazil reproduced with permission of SuperStock (© Steve Vidler, © Yadid Levy/age fotostock).

Every effort has been made to contact copyright holders of material reproduced in this book. Any omissions will be rectified in subsequent printings if notice is given to the publisher.

Contents

About South America 4

Famous places 6

Geography 8

Weather 12

Animals .14

Plants .16

Natural resources and products 18

People .20

Culture and sport 22

Countries 24

Cities and countryside 26

Fun facts 28

Quiz 29

Glossary 30

Find out more 31

Index 32

Some words are shown in bold, **like this**. You can find out what they mean by looking in the glossary.

About South America

A **continent** is a huge area of land. There are seven continents on Earth. This book is about the continent of South America. South America is the fourth biggest continent.

ARCTIC OCEAN

North America

Europe

Asia

ATLANTIC OCEAN

Africa

PACIFIC OCEAN

Equator

South America

INDIAN OCEAN

PACIFIC OCEAN

Australia

SOUTHERN OCEAN

Antarctica

South America is mostly surrounded by sea. To the west is the Pacific Ocean. To the east is the Atlantic Ocean. A narrow strip of land links South America to the continent of North America.

South America fact file	
Area	17,813,938 square kilometres (6,878,000 square miles)
Population	around 400 million
Number of countries	12
Highest mountain	Aconcagua at 6,959 metres (22,831 feet)
Longest river	Amazon at about 6,437 kilometres (4,000 miles)

Famous places

There are many famous places in South America. Some are ancient. Machu Picchu is a ruined city high up in the Andes Mountains in Peru. It was built by the Inca people more than 500 years ago.

Tourists can visit the ruins of Machu Picchu high up in the mountains.

The statue's open arms are a sign of peace.

Some famous places are modern. A huge statue of Jesus Christ stands on top of a mountain near the city of Rio de Janeiro in Brazil. It is almost 40 metres (130 feet) tall and was built between 1922 and 1931.

Geography

South America has **grasslands**, rainforests, rivers, deserts, and mountains. The Andes is the world's longest **mountain range**. It runs for about 7,250 kilometres (4,505 miles) along the west coast of the **continent**.

Mount Cotopaxi in the Andes is an active volcano.

Sechura
Desert

Andes
Mountains

Atacama
Desert

Mount
Aconcagua

| 0 | 500 miles |
| 0 | 800 km |

The Amazon rainforest is the biggest rainforest in the world.

Tropical rainforests cover about one-third of South America. The largest is the Amazon rainforest, which grows along the banks of the River Amazon in Brazil.

The mighty River Amazon is the longest river in South America. It is the second longest river on Earth. It begins in the Andes Mountains in Peru and flows across Peru and Brazil to the Atlantic Ocean.

The Amazon River flows into the sea off the coast of Brazil.

Angel Falls
Lake Guatavita
Amazon River
Sao Francisco River
Lake Titicaca
Lake Poopó
Uruguay River
Lake Chiquita
Lake Mirim
Negro River

0	500 miles
0	800 km

Lake Buenos Aires

Reeds make good materials for making boats on Lake Titicaca.

South America has many large lakes. Lake Titicaca is high up in the Andes Mountains. Tall **reeds** grow around the edges of the lake. Local people use the reeds to make huts and fishing boats.

Weather

South America has many different types of weather. It is hot and wet in the rainforests. The **grasslands** are hot and dry. It is even drier in the desert. Parts of the Atacama Desert in Chile have never had any rain.

The Atacama Desert is one of the driest places on Earth.

Ice and glaciers are found in the cold south of South America.

High up in the mountains, the weather gets very cold. It is also cold and windy at the southern tip of South America. In the winter, temperatures there can fall as low as -33 degrees Celsius (-27 degrees Fahrenheit).

Animals

An amazing number of animals live in South America. Andean **condors** soar above the mountains. Giant anteaters roam the **grasslands**. Huge tortoises live on the Galapagos Islands, off the west coast of Ecuador.

The Galapagos Islands are famous for their unusual wildlife.

Jaguars live in the Amazon rainforest. They are fierce hunters.

The Amazon rainforest is home to thousands of types of animals, such as jaguars, **capybaras**, and **anacondas**. There are also birds, lizards, monkeys, frogs, and insects. Many rainforest animals live in the treetops, where there is plenty of food to eat.

Plants

Many unusual plants grow in South America. The puya raimondii is a very rare plant that grows in the Andes Mountains. It only flowers once in its life, when it is between about 80 to 150 years old. Then the plant dies.

Puya raimondii flowers bloom on a giant stalk, which can be 10 metres (33 feet) tall.

roots

Orchid roots dangle
down and collect
water from the air.

Tall trees, such as brazil nut trees, grow in the
rainforest. Beautiful orchids live high on the tree
branches. Long vines twist around their trunks.

Natural resources and products

South America has many **natural resources**. In Argentina, the **grasslands** are used for farming. Farmers grow crops and keep cattle and sheep. These farms are some of the biggest in the world.

Huge herds of cattle graze on the grassland in Argentina.

This miner from Colombia is holding an emerald dug from the ground.

Many valuable products come from the rainforest, such as wood, brazil nuts, and palm oil. Oil comes from Venezuela. Copper and iron **ore** are **mined** in Chile. Colombia has coal mines and also produces precious emeralds.

19

People

About 380 million people live in South America. Some are **descended from** Europeans who settled in South America in the 1500s. Some are descended from people who lived in South America before the Europeans arrived.

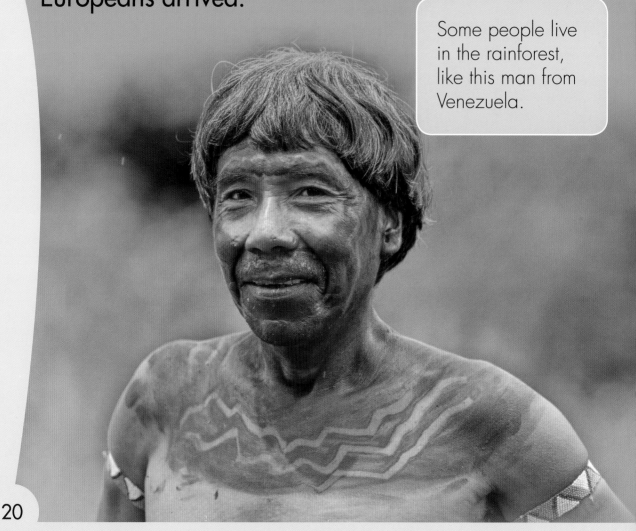

Some people live in the rainforest, like this man from Venezuela.

This sign from Argentina is in Spanish.

Most people in South America speak Spanish. In Brazil, people speak Portuguese. Many ancient South American languages are also spoken. One of these is Quechua, which was the language of the Inca people.

Culture and sport

Sport is very popular in South America, especially football. Brazil has won the football World Cup a record five times. Rio de Janeiro, in Brazil, is the home of the 2016 summer Olympic Games.

These footballers are playing in the 2011 Copa America football tournament.

Carnival time in Rio is the highlight of the year!

Every year, in February or March, a world-famous carnival is held in Rio de Janeiro. Millions of people take part or go to watch. The streets are filled with brilliantly decorated floats and dancers dressed in spectacular costumes.

Countries

There are 12 countries in South America. There are also two small **territories** – French Guiana and the Falkland Islands.

CARIBBEAN SEA

Guyana
Venezuela
Suriname
Colombia
French Guiana

Ecuador

Brazil

Peru

Bolivia

PACIFIC OCEAN

Paraguay

ATLANTIC OCEAN

Uruguay

Chile

Argentina

N
W   E
S

0   500 miles
0   800 km

This map shows the countries and territories of South America.

The Falkland Islands

This photograph shows the government building in Brasilia, the capital of Brazil.

Brazil is the biggest country in South America. It is also the fifth largest country in the world. The smallest country in South America is Suriname. Brazil is about 50 times bigger than Suriname.

Cities and countryside

In South America there are many cities where large numbers of people live. Among the biggest are São Paulo in Brazil and Buenos Aires in Argentina. São Paulo is busy and crowded. It has many modern buildings. It also has many **slums** where very poor people live.

Skyscrapers tower over the city of São Paulo, Brazil.

These children live in an Aymara village in a remote part of Peru.

Life in the countryside is very different. For example, the Aymara people live in villages in the Andes Mountains in Bolivia, Chile, and Peru. Often, the villages have no electricity or running water.

Fun facts

- Angel Falls in Venezuela is the world's highest waterfall. The water plunges 979 metres (3,212 feet) down.

- About three-quarters of South America lies to the south of the **equator**.

- The Amazon rainforest in Brazil is about the same size as Australia.

- Lake Titicaca in Bolivia is the highest lake that boats can sail on.

Quiz

1. Which people built Machu Picchu in the Andes Mountains?

2. Which country in South America is very long and thin?

3. What is the world's longest mountain range?

4. What is the largest rainforest in South America?

Glossary

anaconda huge snake that lives in the rainforest

capybara animal that looks like a huge guinea pig

condor large bird that flies over mountains

continent one of seven huge areas of land on Earth

descended from related to someone long ago

equator imaginary line running around the middle of Earth

grasslands very large area of land covered in grasses

mined dug up from under the ground

mountain range long line of mountains

natural resources natural materials that we use, such as wood, coal, oil, and rock

ore rocks that contain metals

reeds tall grasses, which grow in water or marshy land

slums overcrowded area of a city where poor people live

territories lands that are controlled by another country, far away

tropical place near the equator where the weather is hot and rainy all year

Find out more

Books

Horrible Geography of the World, Anita Ganeri (Scholastic, 2010)

Oxford First Atlas (OUP, 2010)

South America (Exploring Continents), Anita Ganeri (Heinemann Library, 2008)

Websites to visit

kids.discovery.com/tell-me/people-and-places/our-7-continents
Games, puzzles, and activities about the seven continents can be found on this website.

kids.nationalgeographic.com/kids/games/geographygames/copycat
This fun game helps you to find the continents on a map of the world.

www.worldatlas.com
This site has lots of maps, facts, and figures about continents.

Index

Amazon 5, 9, 10, 15, 28
Andes Mountains 6, 8, 10, 11, 16, 27
Angel Falls 28
animals 14–15
area of South America 5
Argentina 18, 21, 26
Atacama Desert 12
Atlantic Ocean 5, 10

Bolivia 27, 28
Brazil 7, 9, 10, 21, 22, 23, 25, 26, 28

Carnival 23
Chile 12, 19, 27
cities 7, 23, 25, 26
Colombia 19
continents 4
countries 5, 24–25
countryside 27
culture 23

deserts 12

equator 28

famous places 6–7
farming 18

Galapagos Islands 14
geography 8–11
grasslands 12, 14, 18

Inca people 6, 21

Jesus Christ, statue of 7

lakes 11
languages 21

Machu Picchu 6
mining 19
mountains 5, 6, 7, 8, 10, 11, 13, 16

natural resources 18

Pacific Ocean 5
people 20–21
Peru 6, 10, 27
plants 16–17
population 5
products 19

rainforests 9, 12, 15, 17, 19, 28
Rio de Janeiro 7, 22, 23
rivers 5, 9, 10

São Paolo 26
sport 22
Suriname 25

territories 24
Titicaca, Lake 11, 28
tourism 6

Venezuela 19, 28
volcanoes 8

weather 12–13